THE

LAST FRENCH POST

IN

THE VALLEY OF THE UPPER MISSISSIPPI,

NEAR FRONTENAC, MINN.;

WITH NOTICES OF ITS COMMANDANTS.

BY

EDWARD D. NEILL.

SAINT PAUL, MINN.:
THE PIONEER PRESS COMPANY.
1887.

"They who make researches into antiquity may be said to pass often through many dark lobbies and dusky places, before they come to the *Aula lucis*, the great hall of light; they must repair to old archives, and peruse many moulded and moth-eaten records, and so bring light as it were from darkness, to inform the present world what the former did, and make us see truth through our ancestors' eyes."—HOWELL'S "*Londinopolis*," London, A. D. 1657.

FRENCH POST,

LAKE PEPIN, MINNESOTA.

The recent discovery of two cannon balls, one of six-pound and the other of four-pound calibre, at Frontenac station, near Lake Pepin, Minn., renders desirable a notice of the last French establishment in the valley of the upper Mississippi river.

The department of trade called "La Baye" included all the French posts between Green Bay and the Falls of Saint Anthony. Bellin, the distinguished geographer in "Remarques sur la carte de l'Amerique Septentrionale," published in 1755, at Paris, refers to those on the shores of the river Mississippi and its tributaries, and mentions "Fort St. Nicholas at the mouth of the Wisconsin;" a small fort at the entrance of Lake Pepin; one above, on the opposite side of the lake; and another on the largest isle just above the lake, built in 1695, by Le Sueur. Nicholas Perrot, when commandant of the "La Baye" district, in the autumn of 1685, ascended the Mississippi and passed the winter at "Montagne qui tremps dans l'eau," just beyond Black river, according to Franquelin's map, and subsequently built the fort on the east side of the lake, on the same map marked "Fort St. Antoine." In 1689 Le Sueur was one of his associates at Lake Pepin; and Boisguillot, for a time in charge at Mackinaw, then at the post on the Mississippi just above the mouth of the Wisconsin.

The first calling of the lake, as Pepin appears in the journal of Le Sueur in 1700, and was perhaps given to the sheet of water in compliment to Monsieur Pepin[1] who, in 1679, was with Du Luth on the shores of Lake Superior, or some other member of that Canadian family.

---

1. Stephen Pepin, the Sieur de la Fond, married Marie Boucher, the aunt of the Sieur de la Perriere.

4

After the year 1703, owing to the hostility of the Renards (Fox Indians), the French abandoned all their existing posts in the "La Baye" district of the upper Mississippi, and, with the exception of a few lawless voyageurs left the country. By the treaty of Utrecht, in 1713, France yielded to Great Britain all the country around Hudson's bay, and after this the former power turned its attention to the region west of Lake Superior and the discovery of a route to the Western ocean. In July, 1717, Lieutenant La Noue[1] was ordered to establish a post at the extremity of Lake Superior, and to explore the chain of lakes westward, and Captain Paul Saint Pierre[2] in 1718, was ordered to Chagouamigon bay and Lake Superior. Pachot, an ensign, at the same time was sent to the Sioux to persuade them to make peace with the Cristinaux. Soon after Pachot's return to Saint Pierre's post at Chagouamigon, the Sioux attacked the Indians near Kamanistigouya[3] and killed seventeen, which so alarmed the Saulteurs (Ojibways) of Chagouamigon bay that they began to prepare to go to war against the Sioux. Saint Pierre directed the officers, Pachot and Linctot, to visit the Sioux and censure them for their hostility to the Cristinaux, but they found that they had formed an alliance with the Renards (Foxes), and were implacable.

Pachot in a letter to the French government, dated Quebec, Oct. 27, 1722, suggested that as the Sioux were hostile to the Lake Superior tribes, a trading post for their benefit should be established near the Falls of St. Anthony, and that the officer of the post with the traders' canoes should first proceed to Chagouamigon bay, and then to the Neouissakouete (Bois Brulé) river. At that period the "Outabatonha," or "Scioux of the Rivers," dwelt in the valley of the Saint Croix river, fifteen leagues below Snake river. Charlevoix, a learned Jesuit, in 1721, under the auspices of the French government, visited Canada and Louisiana, and upon his return urged the establishment of a trading post and sending two missionaries among the Sioux to learn the language, in the belief that through their country a route to the Pacific ocean could be discovered. His suggestions were favor-

1. Killed in 1734, by a band of Iroquois.
2. Captain Paul Legardeur, Saint Pierre was the son of J. Baptiste Legardeur, who on the eleventh of July, 1656, married Marguerite, the daughter of the brave explorer, Jean Nicolet, the first white man who in 1634-5 visited Green Bay and vicinity in Wisconsin.
3. Also written Gamanetygoya and Kamanistigoya. Baraga in his Ojibway dictionary defines Ningitawitigweiag as the place where a river divides into several branches.

ably considered but delay ensued in carrying out the project, by the hostility of the Renards, who had killed several Frenchmen, and also refused to allow traders to pass to the Sioux through their country. De Lignery was therefore dispatched, in 1726, to confer with the tribes near Green Bay, and on the seventh of June made a treaty with the chiefs of the Renards (Foxes), Sakis (Sauks) and Puans (Winnebagoes).

The way now being opened, a company to trade with the Sioux was formed, and among the associates were Jean Baptiste Boucher, the Sieur de Montbrun, Francois Boucher de Montbrun, and Francois Campeau. Campeau was a blacksmith and armorer and in the articles of agreement it was provided that upon the payment of four hundred livres in coin or peltries he could work for any who might wish his services.

The commandant appointed to conduct the expedition was René Boucher, the Sieur de la Perriere,[1] and a relative of two of the trading company. The chaplains attached were the Jesuits Louis Ignatius Guignas and De Gonor. They left Montreal on the sixteenth of June, 1727, and on the seventeenth of September reached the enlargement of the Mississippi, the picturesque Lake Pepin. Immediately René Boucher, the Sieur de la Perriere, selected a site upon a low point, about the middle of the lake shore, opposite Maiden's Rock and ordered the erection of a stockade of pickets, each twelve feet in length, forming a square of one hundred feet, with two bastions. Within the enclosure was a log house for the commandant, a residence for the missionaries, and a storehouse,[2] all of which by the last

---

1. The Boucher family was one of the most distinguished in Canada.

Children of Gaspard, the immigrant:

Pierre, governor of Three Rivers.

Marie, wife of Stephen Pepin.

Children of Pierre of Three Rivers:

Pierre,   born A. D. 1653.

Marie,   "   "   1655; married René Gualtier Varennes.

Jean,   "   "   1667; Sieur Montbrun.

Rene,   "   "   1668;   " de la Perriere.

J. Baptiste, "   "   1673;   " de Niverville.

Children of René:

Tanguay gives as children of René:

René, born Jan. 10, 1699.

Jean Baptiste, born Aug. 10, 1700.

François, born July 14, 1704.

2 The houses were all sixteen feet in width. One was twenty-five feet, one thirty feet, and the third, thirty-eight feet long.

of October was completed. The fort was named "Beauharnois," in compliment to the governor of Canada; and the missionaries called their mission "St. Michael the Archangel." Father Guignas in a letter from the fort writes:[1] "The fourth of the month of November we did not forget that it was the Saint's Day of the general. The holy mass was said for him in the morning, and they were well prepared to celebrate in the evening, but the slowness of the pyrotechnists and the variableness of the weather led to the postponement of the celebration to the fourteenth of the same month, when they shot off some very beautiful rockets, and made the air resound with a hundred shouts of 'Vive le Roy' and of 'Vive Charles de Beauharnois.' * * * * That which contributed a great deal to the merry making was the fright of some Indians. When these poor people saw the fireworks in the air, and the stars fall from the sky, the women and children fled, and the more courageous of the men cried for mercy, and earnestly begged that we would stop the astonishing play of that terrible medicine (medecin)."

On the fifteenth of April, 1728, the water rose so high in the lake that for several weeks it was necessary to abandon the fort. During the spring the commandant ascended the Mississippi, for sixty leagues, but found no Sioux, as they had gone to war against the Mahas, toward the Missouri. The missionary De Gonor left at this time, and when he reached Mackinaw on his way to Montreal, found there Pierre Gualtier Varennes,[2] the Sieur Verendrye (Verandrie), who had been in command at Lake Nepigon and desired to seek for the western ocean by way of Lake Winnipeg.

A year after the expedition of Sieur de la Perriere, on the fifth of June, 1728, the Sieur de Lignery left Montreal with a force to punish the Renards (Foxes), who continued to molest traders. During the night of the seventeenth of August he reached Green Bay, and the next day at midnight arrived at the mouth of Fox river, where Fort St. Francis[3] was situated. The Renards fled at the approach of the

1. Margry. Vol. VI.
2. His mother was a sister of Boucher de la Perriere. He was a cadet in 1697, and in 1704 served in an expedition to New England, and the next year was in New Foundland. Desirous of distinction, he went to France and was connected with a Bretagne regiment. He attracted attention by his bravery at Malplaquet, in September, 1709, where the Duke of Marlborough defeated the French. After he returned to Canada he had the rank of ensign.
3. Fort St. Francis is the name given in Crespel's *Voyages.*

army, abandoning everything in their villages, and retreating to the country of the Aioues (Ioway), beyond the Mississippi. On the twenty-fourth of the month he reached the village of the Puans (Winnebagoes), who had also run away. Upon his return he burned Fort St. Francis, lest the Renards should return, take possession, and make war upon the Folles Avoines, who were allies of the French. De Beaujeu was the second in command of this expedition, and was not satisfied with De Lignery's conduct.

On account of the hostility of the Indians, the post on Lake Pepin, in October, 1728, was left in charge of a youth twenty years old, Christopher Dufrost,[1] the Sieur de la Jemeraye; and twelve persons, among whom were the Sieur de Boucherville, Jean Baptiste Boucher, the Sieur Montbrun, and the Jesuit Guignas, embarked with their goods, in canoes, for Montreal, by way of the Illinois river, as the hostility of the Foxes prevented the route by the Wisconsin. On the twelfth of the month, twenty-two leagues above the Illinois river, they were captured by the Mascoutens and Kickapoos, who were allies of the Foxes.

Among the manuscript in the Parliament library of Canada, at Ottawa, there is a communication of De Tilly, dated April 29, 1729, which mentions that " eleven Frenchmen and Father Guignase having left the Fort Pepin to descend the river Mississippi as far as the Illinois, and to go from thence to Canada, were captured by the Mascoutens and Quicapous, and brought to the Riviere au Boeuf, with the intention to deliver them to the Renards, and that the Sieur de Montbrun and his brother, with another Frenchman, escaped from their hands the night before they were to be surrendered to these Indians. The Sieur de Montbrun left his brother sick among the Tamaroides,[2] and brought the intelligence to M. le General, avoiding certain posts on the way to escape the Mascoutens and Quicapous."

Governor Beauharnois, on the twenty-ninth of October, wrote to the French Government: " I have the honor to report, upon what has passed upon the part of the Kickapoos and Mascoutens who arrested the French coming from the post of the Sioux, and the enterprise of Sieur de Montbrun, after his escape from the village of the savages

1. He was the son of a naval officer who in 1698 was in command at Fort Frontenac. His mother's maiden name was Marie Gualtier, and on Dec. 7, 1707, he was born.

2. The Tamarois were a band of the Illinois Indians.

8

to bring us the news of the affair. He is a person zealous in the service of his majesty, and I can not refuse the request he has made to write to you to procure his promotion. He is cadet of the troop and a most excellent officer.

The Sieur de la Jemeraye, who remained among the Sioux with some Frenchmen, left Lake Pepin and brought the Renards' chief[1] to the River St. Joseph[2] also deserves your protection."

Boucherville and Guignas remained prisoners for several months, and the former did not reach Detroit until June, 1729. The account of expenditures made during his captivity is interesting as showing the value of merchandise at that time. It reads as follows:

"Memorandum of the goods that Monsieur de Boucherville was obliged to furnish in the service of the king, from the time of his detention among the Kickapoos, on the twelfth of October, 1728, until his return to Detroit, in the year 1729, in the month of June. On arriving at the Kickapoo village, he made a present to the young men to secure their opposition to some evil minded old warriors—

Two barrels of powder, each fifty pounds at Montreal price, valued at the sum of.. 150 liv.
One hundred pounds of lead and balls making the sum of...... 50 liv.
Four pounds of vermilion, at 12 francs the pound................. 48fr.
Four coats, braided, at twenty francs................................ 80fr.
Six dozen knives at four francs the dozen........................... 24fr.
Four hundred flints, one hundred gun-worms, two hundred ramrods and one hundred and fifty files, the total at the maker's prices... 90 liv.

After the Kickapoos refused to deliver them to the Renards (Foxes) they wished some favors, and I was obliged to give them the following which would allow them to weep over and cover their dead:

Two braided coats @ 20 fr. each...................................... 40fr.
Two woolen blankets @ 15 fr... 30
One hundred pounds of powder @ 30 sous........................... 75
One hundred pounds of lead @ 10 sous.............................. 25
Two pounds of vermilion @ 12 fr...................................... 24

1. Governor Beauharnois, in a communication dated May 6, 1730, alludes to the defeat of the Renards by the allied Menomonees, Ojibways and Winnebagos, and writes: "It is also confirmed by the journey taken since this last adventure by the great chief of the Renards to the River St. Joseph."
2. In Michigan.

Moreover, given to the Renards to cover their dead and prepare them for peace, fifty pounds of powder, making......... 75fr.

One hundred pounds of lead @ 10 sous............................ 50

Two pounds of vermilion @ 12 fr...................................... 24

During the winter a considerable party was sent to strike hands
with the Illinois.   Given at that time:

Two blue blankets @ 15 fr................................... 30

Four men's shirts @ 6 fr................................ 24

Four pairs of long-necked bottles @ 6 fr............................ 24

Four dozen of knives @ 4 fr........ 16

Gun-worms, files, ramrods, and flints, estimated.................... 40

Given to engage the Kickapoos to establish themselves upon a
neighboring isle, to protect from the treachery of the Renards—

Four blankets @ 15fr.. 60f.

Two pairs of bottles, 6fr.. 24

Two pounds of vermilion, 12fr... 24

Four dozen butcher knives, 6fr.. 24

Two woolen blankets @ 15fr............................. 30

Four pairs of bottles @ 6fr................................ 24

Four shirts @ 6fr... 24

Four dozen of knives @ 4fr.. 16

The Renards having betrayed and killed their brothers, the Kickapoos, I seized the favorable opportunity, and to encourage the latter
to avenge themselves, I gave—

Twenty-five pounds of powder, @ 30 sous............................ 37f.10s.

Twenty-five pounds of lead, @ 10s................................... 12f.10s.

Two guns at 30 livres each............................ .... 60f.

One-half pound of vermillion .... 6f.

Flints, guns, worms and knives.. 20f.

The Illinois coming to the Kikapoos village, I supported them
at my expense, and gave them powder, balls and shirts val-
ued at...... .... 50f.

In departing from the Kickapoos village, I gave them the
rest of the goods for their good treatment, estimated at...... 80f.

In dispatches sent to France, in October, 1729, by the Canadian
gvernment, the following reference is made to Fort Beauharnois:
"They agree that the fort built among the Scioux, on the border of
Lake Pepin, appears to be badly situated on account of the freshets,

*2

but the Indians assure that the water rose higher than it ever did before, and this is credible inasmuch as it did not reach the fort this year [1729]. When Sieur de la Perriere located it at that place it was on the assurance of the Indians that the waters did not rise so high; however, he could not locate it more advantageously in regard both to the quantity of land suitable for cultivation, and to the abundance of game. * * * As the water might possibly rise as high, this fort could be removed four or five arpents from the lake shore without prejudice to the views entertained in building it on its present site.

"It is very true that these Indians did leave shortly after on a hunting excursion, as they are in the habit of doing, for their own support and that of their families, who have only that means of livelihood, as they do not cultivate the soil at all. M. de Beauharnois has just been informed that their absence was occasioned only by having fallen in while hunting with a number of prairie Scioux, by whom they were invited to accompany them on a war expedition against the Mahas, which invitation they accepted, and returned only in the month of July following.

"The interests of religion, of the service, and of the colony, are involved in the maintenance of this establishment, which has been the more necessary as there is no doubt but the Foxes, when routed, would have found an asylum among the Scioux had not the French been settled there, and the docility and submission manifested by the Foxes can not be attributed to any cause except the attention entertained by the Scioux for the French, and the offers which the former made the latter, of which the Foxes were fully cognizant.

"It is necessary to retain the Scioux in these favorable dispositions, in order to keep the Foxes in check, and counteract the measures they might adopt to gain over the Scioux, who will invariably reject their propositions so long as the French remain in the country, and their trading post shall continue there. But, despite all these advantages and the importance of preserving that establishment, M. de Beauharnois can not take any steps until he has news of the French who asked his permission this summer to go up there with a canoe load of goods, and until assured that those who wintered there have not dismantled the fort, and that the Scioux continue in the same sentiments. Besides, it does not seem very easy, in the present conjuncture, to maintain that post unless there is a solid peace with the Foxes; on the other hand, the greatest portion of the traders who applied in 1727 for the establishment of that post have withdrawn, and will not send thither any more, as the rupture with the Foxes, through whose country it is necessary to pass in order to reach the Scioux in canoe, has led them to abandon the idea. But the one and the other case might be remedied. The Foxes will, in all probability, come or send next year to sue for peace; therefore, if it be granted to them on advantageous conditions, there need be no apprehension when going to the Scioux, and another company could be formed, less numerous than the first, through whom, or some responsible merchants able to afford the outfit, a new treaty could be made, whereby these difficulties would be soon obviated. One only trouble remains, and that is, to send a commanding and sub-officer and some soldiers up there, which are absolutely necessary for the maintenance of good order at that post; the missionaries would not go there without a commandant. This article, which regards the service, and the expense of which must be on his majesty's account, obliges them to apply for orders. They will, as far as lies in their power, induce the traders to meet that expense, which will possibly amount to 1,000 livres or 1,500 livres a year for the commandant, and in proportion for the officer under him; but, as in the beginning of an establishment the expenses exceed the profits, it is improbable that any company of merchants will assume the outlay, and in this case they demand orders on this point, as well as his majesty's opinion as to the necessity of preserving so useful a post, and a nation which has already afforded proofs of its fidelity and attachment."

The Canadian authorities determined to send an expedition against the insolent Renards and their allies. In March, 1730, the Sieur Marin then in command among the Folles Avoines (Menomonees), with a number of friendly Indians, moved against the Renards and had an engagement of the "warmest character." During the month of September of the same year a force under Sieur de Villiers vanquished the tribe, and the French government was informed that "two hundred of their warriors have been killed on the spot, or burned after having been taken as slaves, and six hundred women and children were destroyed."

After the victory over the Renards steps were taken to rebuild the post on a more elevated spot near the first site on Lake Pepin. In

June, 1731, Sieur Linctot was appointed commandant, and Sieur Portneuf was the next officer in rank. Among those now interested in trade with the Sioux were Francis Campeau, Joseph and Pierre Le Duc, and the son of Linctot, a cadet. A new stockade was ordered to be constructed one hundred and twenty feet square, with four bastions, and accommodations within for the commandant.

Linctot passed the winter of 1731–2 at Perrot's first establishment '' Montagne qui trempe dans léau.'' In the spring he ascended to the site of the post ou Sandy Point, where he found a large number of Sioux who expressed satisfaction at the return of the French.

Upon the sixteenth of September, 1733, the Renards (Foxes) and Sakis (Sauks) appeared at Green Bay, but were put to flight by the son of Sieur de Villiers. The Sioux and Ayouais (Ioway) refused to protect them and they were obliged to descend the "Ouapsipinckam" river, which flows into the Mississippi above Rock Island.

Black Hawk, the celebrated Sauk chief captured in 1832, told his biographer that his people moved to that vicinity about one hundred years before, and that in 1768 he was born.

At the request of the elder Linctot he was relieved of the command opposite Maiden Rock, Lake Pepin, and in 1735, Legardeur Saint Pierre took command. In a communication dated twelfth of October, 1736, by the Canadian authorities, is the following: "In regard to the Scioux, Saint Pierre, who commanded at that post, and Father Guignas, the missionary, have written to Sieur de Beauharnois on the tenth and eleventh of last April, that these Indians appeared well intentioned toward the French, and had no other fear than that of being abandoned by them. Sieur de Beauharnois annexes an extract of these letters, and although the Scioux seem very friendly, the result only can tell whether this fidelity is to be absolutely depended upon, for the unrestrained and inconsistent spirit which composes the Indian character may easily change it. They have not come over this summer as yet, but M. de la St. Pierre is to get them to do so next year, and to have an eye on their proceedings."

Upon the sixth of May, 1736, one hundred and forty Sioux arrived at the fort, and said they were taking back to the Puans a slave who had fled to them. Saint Pierre told them that he thought it was a large guard for one woman, and they then alleged that they were going to hunt turkeys to obtain feathers for their arrows. Contin-

uing their journey down the Mississippi, they met and scalped two
Frenchmen. When Saint Pierre was on a visit up the river to see
about building another post, the lawless party returned, and for four
days danced the scalp dance in the vicinity of the fort.

Two canoes of Saulteaux (Ojibways) arrived from La Pointe, Lake
Superior, on the twenty-third of August with letters from Nolan,
Legros and Bourassa, conveying the startling news that the Sioux of
the Woods with a few of the Sioux of the Prairies had killed a number of Verendrye's exploring party, at the Lake of the Woods.

On the fifteenth of August, 1731, arrived at the Grand Portage,
near Pigeon river, the northeastern extremity of Minnesota, on the
shore of Lake Superior, Pierre Gualtier Varennes, the Sieur Verendrye (Verandrie), with an expedition in search of a route to the Pacific ocean. The second in command was his nephew, the brave
youth Christopher Dufrost, the Sieur de la Jemeraye, who for a time
was in charge of Fort Beauharnois. During the autumn, by difficult
portages the Sieur de la Jemeraye and two sons of Verendrye reached
Rainy Lake, and established a trading post, called Fort St. Pierre.

About the middle of July, 1732, Fort St. Pierre was left, and the ex-
plorers ascended to the Lake of the Woods, where they erected Fort
St. Charles. During the year 1733 the Sieur de la Jemeraye went to
Montreal to attend to his uncle's business, and in the beginning of
March a party, conducted by the eldest son of Verendrye, moved
westward and established Fort Maurepas, near the entrance to Lake
Winnipeg, which in September, 1735, was in charge of Sieur de la
Jemeraye, who had returned, and during the following winter two
sons of Verendrye remained there. During the spring of 1736 Jemeraye died at the post. Upon the eighth of June Auneau, the chaplain,
and one of the sons of Verendrye, with some voyageurs, left the post
on the shore of the Lake of the Woods to go to Mackinaw, and while
encamped upon an island in the lake, seven leagues from Fort St.
Charles, they were surprised by the Sioux, and the whole party of
twenty-one killed. Some days after, five voyageurs stopped at the
island, and found the Jesuit chaplain, Auneau, with an arrow in his
brain. The son of Verendrye was lying upon his back, and his flesh
hacked by tomahawks. His head had been removed and was orna-
mented with garters and bracelets of porcupine quills.

The sixteenth of September there came to the Lake Pepin post ten

Indians, three chiefs, and two young slaves, bringing a quantity of beaver skins, which they delivered to Saint Pierre as a pledge of friendship, and declared that they had no part in the attack at the Lake of the Woods. They were then asked as to their knowledge of the killing of two Frenchmen on the Mississippi. The next day a chief came with three young men, one of whom wore in his ear a silver pendant. When asked by Saint Pierre how he obtained the ornament, he smiled but would not answer. The captain tore it from his ear, and found it was similar to those sold by the traders, and placed him under guard.

Thirty-six men and their families, on the eighteenth of December arrived and passing the Fort, visited some Puans (Winnebagoes) encamped in the vicinity. Ouakantape (Wah-kan-tah-pay) was the chief and quite insolent, and some of the party burned the pickets around the garden of Father Guignas, the chaplain.

The gates of the post were opened about eight o'clock of the morning of the twenty-fourth of January 1737, to admit a wood cart, when some of the Sioux pushed in and defiantly behaved. Upon the twentieth of March thirty Sioux appeared from Fond du Lac Superior where they had scalped an Ojibway, his wife and child. The next May a war party of Ojibways came and wished the Puans to unite with them against the Sioux. While they were parleying, five Sioux came to the Fort to trade, and were protected until night, when they were permitted to leave. An Ojibway lying in an ambush, who spoke Sioux, arose and asked " Who are you?", when the Sioux fired and escaped. In view of the hostility of the Indians, Saint Pierre, after conferring with Sieur Linctot the second in command, Father Guignas, and some others, on the thirteenth of May 1737, burned the post, and descended the Mississippi.

Upon the eighteenth of June, 1738, the Sieur Verendrye left Montreal to continue his discoveries. He arrived at Fort Maurepas on twenty-third of September, and pushed on through Lake Winnipeg, to the mouth of the Assiniboine River, ascending which sixty leagues, on the third of October stopped and built Fort La Reine. A little while before, the eldest son of Verendrye [1] built a post at the mouth of the Assiniboine and Red River of the North, which was soon abandoned. On a map of the tribes, rivers and lakes west of Lake Supe-

---

1. For an account of a tour to the Rocky Mountains by the sons of Verendrye, see *Appendix.*

rior, in 1737, appears Red Lake of Minnesota, the Red River, and the "Bois Fort," the Big Woods.

A few days after Fort La Reine was established, the Sieur de la Marque, whose family name was Marin, arrived with his brother desiring to visit the country of the Mandans.

The Foxes in 1740 again became troublesome, and the post on Lake Pepin was for a time abandoned by the French. A dispatch in 1741 uses this language: "The Marquis de Beauharnois' opinion respecting the war against the Foxes, has been the more readily approved by the Baron de Longeuil, Messieurs De la Chassaigne, La Corne, de Lignery, La Noue, and Duplessis-Fabert, whom he had assembled at his house, as it appears from all the letters that the Count has written for several years, that he has nothing so much at heart as the destruction of that Indian nation, which can not be prevailed on by the presents and the good treatment of the French, to live in peace, notwithstanding all its promises.

" Besides, it is notorious that the Foxes have a secret understanding with the Iroquois, to secure a retreat among the latter, in case they be obliged to abandon their villages. They have one already secured among the Sioux of the prairies, with whom they are allied; so that, should they be advised beforehand of the design of the French to wage war against them, it would be easy for them to retire to the one or the other before their passage could be intersected or themselves attacked in their villages."

In the summer of 1743, a deputation of the Sioux came down to Quebec, to ask that trade might be resumed. Three years after this, four Sioux chiefs came to Quebec, and wished that a commandant might be sent to Fort Beauharnois; which was not granted.

During the winter of 1745–6, De Lusignan visited the Sioux country, ordered by the government to hunt up the "coureurs des bois," and withdraw them from the country. They started to return with him, but learning that they would be arrested at Mackinaw, for violation of law, they ran away. While at the villages of the Sioux of the lakes and plains, the chiefs brought to this officer nineteen of their young men, bound with cords, who had killed three Frenchmen, at the Illinois. While he remained with them they made peace with the Ojibways of La Pointe, with whom they had been at war for some time. On his return, four chiefs accompanied him to Montreal, to solicit pardon for their young braves.

The lessees of the trading post lost many of their peltries that winter in consequence of a fire.

In November, 1745, Legardeur de Saint Pierre, St. Luc de la Corne, Marin and his son left Montreal to attack the English settlements in New York. Passing Fort St. Frederick, at Crown Point, on the thirteenth of the month, by the twenty-seventh, the French and Indians were at Fort Edward. On the next day they crossed Fish creek, a tributary of the Hudson, and the combined forces under the elder Marin, attacked the settlement of Saratoga, killed Capt. Philip Schuyler and many others, took sixty prisoners, and burned nearly all the houses. They then retraced their steps and on the seventh of December returned to Montreal. Upon the thirtieth of the same month Saint Pierre was sent again to Crown Point with a large force to surprise the frontier settlements of New York and New England. He passed the winter in alarming the English, and in April was again in Montreal. During the latter part of the next year he was sent to Mackinaw, whither he was accompanied by his brother Louis Legardeur, the Chevalier de Repentigny.

In 1749 the Sioux earnestly entreated the elder Marin[1] to use his influence with the governor of Canada to re-establish the post at Lake Pepin. The next year Marin was sent to the Sioux, and La Jonquiere, the governor of Canada, directed him to proceed to the source of the Mississippi river to see if some stream could not be discovered, at the height of lands, which flowed toward the western ocean. Marin's son, known as the Chevalier and captain of the military order of St. Louis, the same year that his father went to Lake Pepin, was ordered to "La Pointe de Chagouamigon" of Lake Superior and remained two years, and in 1752 Governor La Jonquiere directed him to relieve his father at the Lake Pepin post, and to prosecute discoveries. He remained here for two years, and on foot journeyed many leagues both in winter and summer. Saint Pierre had been active in the service from the time that he evacuated the post at Lake Pepin. After the death of Sieur Verendrye, in December, 1749, he was commissioned by the governor of Canada to continue the explorations toward the western ocean. He left Montreal in June, 1750, and on

1. Pierre Paul, son of Cæsar Marin, and his wife, who was the daughter of De Callieres, governor of Canada, was born March 19, 1692, and from his youth was distinguished for his boldness and energy. He was married March 21, 1718, to Marie Guyon.

the twenty-ninth of September reached Rainy lake, and in a confer-
ence with the Cristnaux told them that the younger Marin had
been sent to the Sioux, and that he now hoped the war between the
two tribes would cease.

During the winter of 1751 he was at Fort La Réine on the Assiniboine river, on the twenty-ninth of May of that year, sent Boucher
de Niverville, with two canoes and ten men, to ascend the Saskatchewan
and build a post near the Rocky mountains which was called La Jonquiere. The latter part of this year the Assiniboines and other tribes
toward the Rocky mountains showed hostilities to the French, and
Saint Pierre declared that during the thirty-six years he had been
among Indians, he had never witnessed greater perfidy.

Upon the twenty-second of February, 1752, two hundred Assiniboines appeared at Fort La Reine, passed its gates, took possession of
the guard house, and showed a disposition to kill Saint Pierre. During the summer he abandoned the fort, and on the twenty-fifth of July
arrived at the Grand Portage of Lake Superior, south of Pigeon River.
The next winter he passed in the valley of the Red river, where hunting was good. On the twenty-ninth of February, 1753, he received
a letter from Marin's son, who wrote that the Sioux of the rivers and
lakes deplored the attack of the Sioux of the prairies upon the Cristinaux the year before, and they would be pleased to hold a confer-
ence at Mackinaw. This letter was not received by Legardeur Saint
Pierre until the twenty-sixth of May, at the lower part of the river
Ounepik (Winnipeg), and on the twenty-eighth of July he and Boucher
de Niverville came to Grand Portage, below Pigeon river, Lake Superior. The month before, the elder Marin who had returned from
the Sioux country, arrived at Presque Isle, Lake Erie, with an army
of French and Indians to prevent the advance of the English into the
valley of the Ohio river. Cutting a road through the woods of North-
western Pennsylvania to a branch of the Au Bœuf, called by the
English French creek, he in August, built a stockade, with pickets
twelve feet high, and placed before the gate a four-pound cannon,
and in the bastions six-pounders. During the fall he was attacked
with dysentery, and while sick a messenger came from Montreal,
bearing for him the decoration of the cross of the military order of
Saint Louis. He was too ill to wear it, and on the twenty-ninth of
October, died.

The following record[1] has been preserved: "In the year one thousand seven hundred and fifty-three, on the twenty-ninth day of October, at four and a half in the evening, at 'Riviere aux Bœuf,' called Saint Peter, Monsieur Pierre Paul, Esq., Sieur de Marin, chevalier of royal military order of Saint Louis, captain general, and in command of the army of Belle Riviere (Ohio), at the age of sixty-three years, after having received the sacraments of penance, extreme unction, and the viaticum. His remains were interred in the cemetery of said fort, and during the campaign of the Belle Riviere. There were present at his interment Monsieur Repentigny, commander of the above-mentioned army; Messieurs du Muy, lieutenant of infantry; Bonois, lieutenant of infantry; de Simblin, major of the above-mentioned fort; Laforce, guard of the magazine."

The register is signed by a priest of the Recollect Franciscans, chaplain of the fort Fr. Denys Baron.

Saint Pierre arrived at Montreal from the distant west on the seventh day of October, and on the third of November the Marquis du Quesne wrote to the Minister of war in France that he had sent the Sieur de Saint Pierre to succeed Marin in the command of the Army of the Ohio. He did not reach the stockade at French creek until the first week in December, and seven days after his arrival, came young George Washington with a letter from Governor Dinwiddie, of Virginia. After courteous treatment from Saint Pierre for several days he was sent back with the following note:

"SIR: As I have the honor to be here the commander-in-chief, M. Washington delivered to me the letter which you wrote to the commandant of the French troops. I should have been pleased that you had given him order, or that he had been disposed to go to Canada to see our General to whom it better belongs, than to me, to set forth the evidence of the incontestable rights of the King, my master, to the lands along the Ohio, and to refute the pretentions of the King of Great Britain thereto. I shall transmit your letter to M. the Marquis du Quesne. His reply will be law to me, and if he shall order me to communicate with you, you may be assured that I shall not fail to act promptly.

As to the summons you send me to retire, I do not think I am obliged to obey. Whatever may be your instructions, I am here by order of my general, and I beg you not to doubt for a moment but that I am determined to conform with the exactness and resolution

---

1. Lambing's *Fort Duquesne Registers.*

which becomes a good officer. I do not know that in the progress of this campaign anything has passed which can be regarded an act of hostility, or contrary to the treaties between the two crowns, the continuation of which pleases us as much as it does the English. If you had been pleased to enter into particulars as to the facts which caused your complaint, I should have been honored to give as full and satisfactory reply as possible.

I have made it a duty to receive M. Washington with the distinction due on account of your dignity, and his personal worth. I have the honor to be, Monsieur, your very humble and very obedient servant, LEGARDEUR DE SAINT PIERRE.

At the Fort of the River aux Bœufs, the 15 December, 1753.

Eight weeks after the defeat of Braddock, in 1755, commenced another struggle between the troops of England and France. In the advance of the latter, at the head of the Indian allies was Legardeur de Saint Pierre. On the eighth of September a battle took place near the bottom of Lake George. The conflict was desperate, on the side of the English fell Col. Ephraim Williams, the founder of Williams college, Massachusetts; while upon the part of the French Legardeur de Saint Pierre was fatally wounded. His last words were :[1] "Fight on boys, this is Johnson not Braddock."

In 1755, Marin, the son of the commander who died at French creek, Pennsylvania, was again sent by Governor Du Quesne to command the department " La Baye." The next year, with sixty Indians, he was fighting the English in New York, and in 1757 was engaged in the capture of Fort William Henry, and attacked with great boldness Fort Edward. He was also present in 1758, at Ticonderoga.

Louis Legardeur the Chevalier de Repentigny was the brother of Captain Saint Pierre, and, in 1749, an officer under him at Mackinaw. In 1750 he built a trading establishment one hundred and ten feet square, at his own expense at Sault Ste. Marie, and also began a farm. In 1755, he served with his brother at the time of his death, and in 1758 was with Montcalm at Quebec. At the battle of Sillery, 1760, he was at the head of the French centre, and with his brigade resisted the English, the only brigade before whom the foe did not gain an inch. He was taken prisoner in 1762, and two years later visited France. From 1769 to 1778 he was commandant at Isle of Rhé, and then for four years at Guadeloupe. After this he was governor of

1. Stone's Sir Wm. Johnson, vol 1, page 516.

Senegal, Africa, and on the ninth of October, 1786, died in Paris while on furlough.

St. Luc de la Corne took charge of the posts beyond Lake Superior, after Saint Pierre was recalled, and on the third of September, 1757, married Marie the widow of his predecessor.

During the war of the English colonies for independence, La Corne, was in the service of the British king. Thomas Jefferson, in a letter to John Page, of Virginia, dated Philadelphia, Oct. 13, 1775, alludes to him: "Dear Page: We have nothing new from England, or the camp before Boston. By a private letter this day to a gentleman of congress from General Montgomery we learn that our forces before St. John's are 4,000 in number, besides 500 Canadians, the latter of whom have repelled with great intrepidity three different attacks from the fort.

"We apprehend it will not hold out much longer, as Monsieur St. Luc de la Corne, and several other principal inhabitants of Montreal, who have been our great enemies, have offered to make terms. This St. Luc is a great Seigneur amonst the Canadians, and almost absolute with the Indians. He has been our most bitter enemy. He is acknowledged to be the greatest of all scoundrels. To be assured of this I need only to mention to you that he is the ruffian who, during the late war, when Fort William Henry was surrendered to the French and Indians on condition of saving the lives of the garrison, had every soul "murdered in cold blood."

A descendant of one of the commandants at Lake Pepin, however, adhered to the Americans. Depeyster, the British commander at Mackinaw, under date of April 12, 1781, wrote to the Delaware Indians: "Send me that little babbling Frenchman named Monsieur Linctot, he who poisons your ears, one of those who says he can amuse you with words; only send him to me, or be the means of getting him, and I will then put confidence in you. * * * * If you have not the opportunity to bring me the little Frenchman, you may bring me some Virginia prisoners. I am pleased when I see what you call live meat, because I can speak to it and get information."

The post opposite Maiden's Rock, Lake Pepin, was never occupied after the surrender of Canada to the British. The first English troops entered Minnesota by way of Lake Superior. Major Thompson Maxwell, in his journal, mentions that in May, 1762, he arrived at Grand Portage, now in Minnesota, with a few soldiers, as a guard to the goods of traders. Captain Jonathan Carver, the first British traveler in Minnesota, in 1766, observed "the ruins of a French factory where, it is said, Capt. St. Pierre resided, and carried on a very great trade with the Naudowessies before the reduction of Canada."

Lieut. Z. M. Pike, the first officer of the U. S. Army to pass through Lake Pepin, in 1805, reached "Point du Sable" or Sandy Point, on the same day of the same month as La Perriere in 1727 arrived. He writes "The French, under the government of M. Frontenac, drove the Reynards or Ottaquamies from the Wisconsin, and pursued them up the Mississippi, and as a barrier built a stockade on Lake Pepin, on the west shore just below Point du Sable, and, as was generally

the case with that nation blended the military and mercantile professions by making their fort a factory for the Sioux."

The point in the engraving without a house is Sandy Point. A short distance from the point, near the mouth of what Pike on his map calls Sandy Point creek, there is an elevated plateau from which there is an extensive view. There is evidence that there has

been long ago a clearing made there, and as it is the most suitable
spot in the vicinity for a stockade, and visible to any one coming in
a canoe from the direction of Lake City, it was probably the site of
a French post. The Indian trail to the head of the lake ran through
the valley of the creek and passed Frontenac station, where the two
cannon balls were recently found. They may have been buried by
the Indians as "wakan" or supernatural.

APPENDIX.

In an article from the pen of the writer upon Sieur Verendrye and
sons, published in 1875, there were some erroneous inferences. Since
then the itinerary of Verendrye's sons of their journey to the Rocky
mountains has been published, and it is now more easy to trace the
route of the explorers.

On the tenth of April, 1739, Verendrye sent his son, the Chevalier,
to look out for a site for a fifth post, north of La Reine, at the Lake
of the Prairies, which was built and called Fort Dauphin, and at a
later period a sixth post was established at the Saskatchewan (Pas-
koyac) river, and named Fort Bourbon. The father passed the summer of 1740 at Montreal and Quebec, but on the thirteenth of October
returned to Fort La Reine.

The two sons of Verendrye left Fort La Reine on an exploration
toward the Rocky mountains on the twenty-ninth of April, 1742, and
on the twenty-first of May reached the Mandan villages, on the banks
of the Missouri river. Here they rested two months, and from thence
traveled for twenty days west-southwest, probably in the valley of
the Yellowstone river. Moving south-southwesterly about the middle of September they arrived in a village of Beaux Hommes, and remained with them until the ninth of November, when again proceed-
ing south-southwesterly, on the twelfth day they came to a village of
Petite Cerise. From thence they marched to a Pioya village, and con-
tinuing southwesterly arrived at a village of the "Gens des Chevaux,"
which had been destroyed by the Snake Indians. Here guides were
obtained to lead them to the "Gens de l'Arc," and on the eighteenth

23

of November they reached a village of "Gens de la Belle Riviere," and three days later found the Arcs.

From this point they journeyed generally in a southwesterly course, but sometimes moved northwesterly. On the first of January, 1743, the first view of the mountains was obtained. Under the guidance of an Arc chief they marched, and on the twelfth day halted among the mountains, as the Arcs were unwilling to proceed further owing to the hostility of the Snake Indians.

Coquard, a priest who had been associated with Verendrye, mentions that his sons found falls of water, probably the Yellowstone Falls, and that thirty leagues beyond (au-dessus), they found a narrow pass; also between the mountains and the Missouri (Yellowstone tributary?) there is the outlet of a lake.

Bougainville wrote that southwest of the river Wabick or La Coquile, on the banks of La Graisse river are the Hactanes, or Snake tribe who stretch to the base of a chain of mountains which has a northeasterly trend and that south of this is the Karoskiou river or Cerise Peleé, which flows toward California.

An examination of any good modern map will show that the head waters of Green river, a branch of the Colorado which empties into the Gulf of California, rise near Fremont's Peak. Some of the Snake Indians in Texas are still called Hictans.

Returning from the Rocky Mountains, the Verendrye brothers on the ninth of February, 1743, came to the first of the Arc villages, and on the fifteenth of March they met some of the Petite Cerise tribe, and on the nineteenth arrived at their post on the banks of the Missouri. Upon an eminence in the vicinity they placed a lead plate with the arms of the king of France, and over it stones in the form of a pyramid in honor of the governor of Canada. Pursuing a course generally to the northeast, they reached the Mandan country on the eighteenth of May, and on the twenty-seventh passed the Butte in the Assiniboine region. To the joy of their father, the sons reached Fort La Reine on the second of July.

CPSIA information can be obtained
at www.ICGtesting.com
Printed in the USA
LVIC06175628032O
651507LV00033B/1816